WATER and FIBRE

for a healthy body

Angela Royston

www.heinemann.co.uk/library
Visit our website to find out more information about **Heinemann Library** books.

To order:
 Phone 44 (0) 1865 888066
 Send a fax to 44 (0) 1865 314091
 Visit the Heinemann Bookshop at www.heinemann.co.uk/library to browse our catalogue and order online.

First published in Great Britain by Heinemann Library,
Halley Court, Jordan Hill, Oxford
OX2 8EJ, part of Harcourt Education.
Heinemann is a registered trademark of Harcourt
Education Ltd.

Editorial: Jilly Attwood and Jennifer Tubbs
Design: Ron Kamen and Celia Floyd
Illustrations: Geoff Ward
Picture Research: Catherine Bevan, Rosie Garai and
Liz Eddison
Production: Séverine Ribierre

Originated by Ambassador Litho Ltd
Printed in China by Wing King Tong

ISBN 0 431 16713 3
07 06 05 04 03
10 9 8 7 6 5 4 3 2 1

British Library Cataloguing in Publication Data
Royston, Angela
Water and Fibre
613.2'87
A full catalogue record for this book is available from
the British Library.

Acknowledgements
The Publishers would like to thank the following for
permission to reproduce photographs: Corbis: pp. **8**,
15, **22**, **27**, **28** (Sygma/Jean Pierre), **30**, **33**; Gareth
Boden: pp. **5**, **6**, **7**, **12**, **34**, **40**, **41**; Liz Eddison:
pp. **9**, **14**, **32**, **39**, **42**; Photodisc: pp. **38**; SPL:
pp. **18** (Eye of Science), **19** (Biophoto Associates),
29 (Annabelle Bluesky), **31**, **35** (CNRI); Trevor
Clifford: pp. **10**, **24**.

Cover photograph of water and bran flakes,
reproduced with permission of Gareth Boden.

Every effort has been made to contact copyright
holders of any material reproduced in this book. Any
omissions will be rectified in subsequent printings if
notice is given to the Publishers.

Contents

Any words appearing in the text in bold, **like this**, are explained in the glossary.

Why do we need to eat?

You need to eat and drink to stay alive. Most of the food you eat contains **nutrients**, which your body uses to get **energy**, to grow new **cells** and to get the chemicals it needs to work properly. If your body lacks nutrients, you will become ill.

Nutrients

Nutrients are divided into groups, according to what they supply. **Carbohydrates** and **fats** supply energy. **Proteins** supply **amino acids** – the building blocks needed to make new cells and repair old cells. **Vitamins** and **minerals** supply chemicals that the cells need to function properly. Most foods contain a mixture of nutrients, but many are particularly rich in one kind.

Energy foods

Your body uses energy all the time. Running, walking and activities that involve moving around use up more energy than quieter activities, such as thinking, eating and breathing, but even sleeping burns up energy. Most of your energy comes from the carbohydrates and fats that you eat. Carbohydrates include potatoes, rice and food made from wheat, such as bread and pasta. Sugar is also a carbohydrate, so biscuits, cakes and sweets all give you energy.

Fats

Fats come from animals and from plants. Butter, milk and cheese contain quite a lot of animal fat, while margarines and oils are made from plants. The body stores any extra fat you eat as a layer of fat under the skin.

You are what you eat
Your body is composed of the same kind of nutrients that you eat. Muscles are mainly protein, while your bones contain the minerals calcium and phosphorus. Under your skin is a layer of fat that helps to keep you warm.

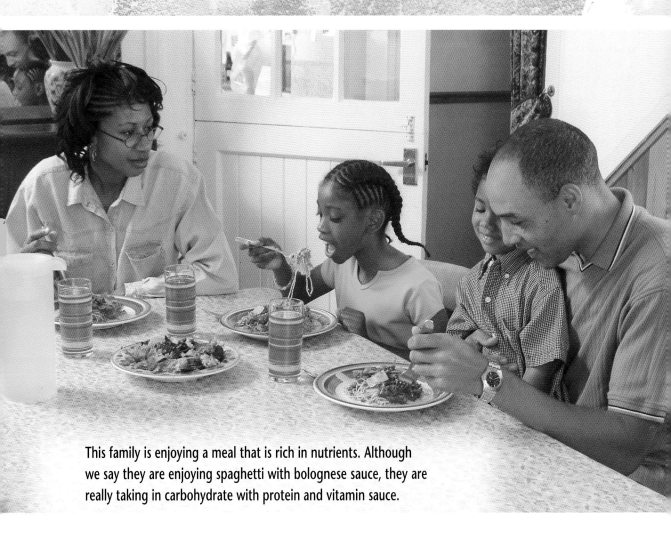

This family is enjoying a meal that is rich in nutrients. Although we say they are enjoying spaghetti with bolognese sauce, they are really taking in carbohydrate with protein and vitamin sauce.

Proteins

Much of your body is made of protein, so, as old cells wear out and die, the body needs constant supplies of new protein to build new cells. While you are still growing, your body needs extra protein to create millions of extra cells. Meat, fish, milk and beans are all good sources of protein.

Vitamins and minerals

Most foods contain small amounts of vitamins and minerals. Minerals include **zinc**, **calcium**, **iron** and **phosphorus**. Fruit and vegetables contain several vitamins and minerals. Milk and cheese contain different ones. Your body only needs small amounts of these chemicals, so, provided you eat a wide range of food, you will get all the vitamins and minerals you need.

Water and fibre

We usually think of healthy food as food that contains plenty of **nutrients**, but this book looks at two essential ingredients that are not nutrients – water and fibre. They are not nutrients because they do not supply **energy**, or help the growth of new **cells**, and they do not contain **vitamins** and **minerals** that the cells need to function. Yet water in particular is essential for us to live, and fibre is necessary to help your body get rid of undigested food and other waste.

Water

About two thirds of your body is water. Body fluids like blood, **urine**, digestive juices and **mucus** are all mainly water. But all cells contain water, so even the parts of the body that look solid, such as muscles, skin and other **organs**, contain water, too.

Body fact
If you weigh 42 kilograms, about 28 kilograms of that is made up of water. This means that your body contains about 28 litres of water.

Losing water

Your body is losing water all the time, mainly through urine and sweat. You need to take in fresh water to replace the water that is lost every day. If you do not drink enough, your body begins to dry out. A person can survive for several weeks without food, but your body quickly becomes **dehydrated** and you would die of thirst after a few days without water.

Drinking plain water is the best way to take in water, but most drinks and many foods contain water, too.

Fibre

Fibre is the parts of plants that your body cannot digest. It consists mainly of the hard walls of plant cells. At one time people thought that fibre was simply waste that the body could do without, but then scientists realized that fibre is needed to keep the digestive system healthy and working well. Fibre helps the body to get rid of **faeces**, that is, solid waste.

The digestive system

The digestive system breaks up food into pieces that are small enough for the nutrients in the food to pass into the blood. Most digestion takes place in the **small intestine**. Any food that is not digested passes through the **large intestine** and collects at the end. It is expelled from your body through the anus when you go to the toilet.

Getting rid of waste

Both water and fibre are important in getting rid of waste. Faeces are easier to expel if they are moist and soft. Fibre absorbs water and so makes the faeces bulkier and softer.

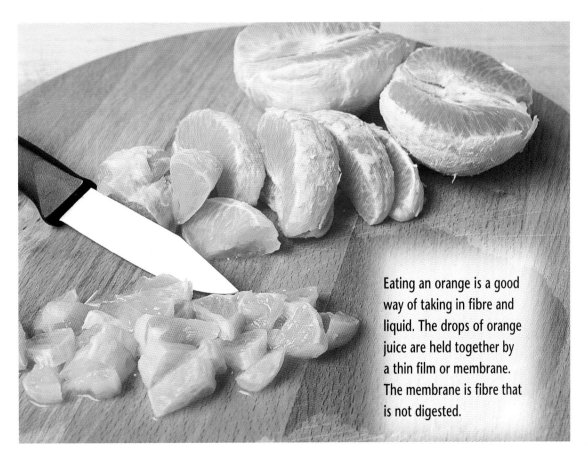

Eating an orange is a good way of taking in fibre and liquid. The drops of orange juice are held together by a thin film or membrane. The membrane is fibre that is not digested.

What is water?

Pure water is made up from just two **elements** – **hydrogen** and **oxygen** – combined together. Both of these elements are normally gases, but when they combine together they form a liquid. Many substances **dissolve** easily in water and so water usually contains other chemicals, too. Some of these chemicals are **minerals** that your body can use. Others are **bacteria** and pollutants that harm your body.

Calcium in water

Some water contains a lot of **calcium**. Calcium is a mineral that makes your bones and teeth strong. The disadvantage is that it makes the water 'hard', and leaves a hard, chalky-white deposit in kettles and in pipes. It takes more soap to get a lather in hard water.

Bacteria in water

Bacteria, like many forms of life, need water to live and breed. Typhoid, cholera and dysentery are three serious illnesses that are carried by water. They are caused by bacteria and kill thousands of people every year. The water you drink must be treated to kill bacteria, this treatment makes it safe to drink.

Tap water

The water that comes out of your taps has been treated before it is piped to homes and other buildings. The **sediments** are removed and filtered out of the water. Then a chemical called chlorine is added to kill any bacteria. In some places the mineral fluoride is added, too. Fluoride protects your teeth from decaying and it is also added to most toothpastes.

Water is treated to make it safe to drink before it is piped to your home.

Water filters

Some people do not like the taste of chlorine in the water. They also worry because chemicals from factories and **pesticides** from farms can seep into the water. Tap water is tested to make sure that it does not contain too many of these harmful chemicals, but many families use water filters to remove the rest. Water filters also remove calcium and chlorine. This makes the water 'softer' and it tastes nicer, too.

Bottled water

Some companies produce bottled water that has been collected from underground springs. Many people think that bottled water tastes better than tap water and does not contain chlorine or other chemicals that are added to tap water. However, bottled water is expensive and many people consider it an unnecessary luxury.

This jug contains a water filter. It removes mercury, zinc, lead and other chemicals that can harm the body.

Water fact

The water you drink is the same water that the dinosaurs drank! The Earth's water is constantly **recycled**. It evaporates from the oceans and falls as rain. Some of the rain runs into reservoirs, wells and underground springs. The rest flows into rivers and back to the oceans.

Water in food

Even solid foods contain a lot of water. This is because all food comes from plants, **fungi** or animals, and, like all living things, they consist mainly of water. Some foods contain more water than others. Leafy vegetables, such as lettuce and watercress, have the most – they are over 90 per cent water.

Plants

Plants take in water from the soil through their roots. **Dissolved** in the water are **nutrients** that the plant needs to remain healthy. The water and nutrients travel through narrow tubes up the stem to the leaves. Here, some of the water combines with **carbon dioxide** from the air to make food, using the **energy** of sunlight. The sugary food is carried to all other parts of the plant – the flowers, fruit, stem, leaves and roots.

Fruit juice

Fruit contains seeds that can grow into new plants. Some plants surround the seeds with sweet, juicy flesh. This kind of fruit contains a lot of water and is often made into fruit juice. The fruit of apples, oranges, pineapples, peaches, mangos and blackcurrants, for example, are squashed and the juice is collected and sold in bottles or cartons.

Vegetable or fruit?
Although we think of cucumbers, aubergines, peppers and tomatoes as vegetables, they are really fruits. You can see the seeds inside them.

You can squeeze oranges to make orange juice. When the squeezing has finished, the only solids left will be the skin, the pith and the seeds.

Other food from plants

Nuts, grains, peas and beans are seeds, too. They contain water, but not as much as juicy fruits. Most vegetables come from other parts of the plant and they are all rich in water. Cabbage, watercress and lettuce are leaves and contain the most water. Broccoli and cauliflowers are flowers, while celery and asparagus are stems. Some plants store food in their roots. Potatoes and onions are two examples of root vegetables. Some vegetables, such as carrots and beetroot, are juiced and sold as drinks.

Food from animals

Meat and fish are more than half water, but meat contains much less water than fruit and vegetables. Female cows, sheep and goats make milk that we drink or make into cheese and yoghurt. Milk is about 90 per cent water, so when you have a drink of milk you are drinking mainly water. The other 10 per cent consists of **fat**, sugar and **protein**, as well as **vitamins** and **minerals**.

Dried food

Sometimes food is dried to preserve it. Raisins and sultanas are different kinds of dried grapes. Even so, these foods still contain some water. Dried dates, for example, are 15 per cent water.

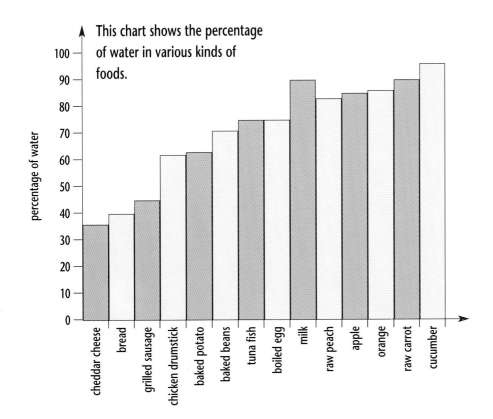

This chart shows the percentage of water in various kinds of foods.

What is fibre?

Fibre is the term given to a mixture of substances, mainly complex **carbohydrates**. These cannot be digested in the **small intestine** in humans, but pass into the **large intestine** where they are fermented. Fibre can be classified as **insoluble**, such as **cellulose**, or **soluble**, such as pectin, depending on whether or not it **dissolves** in ethanol (a type of alcohol).

Insoluble fibre

Cellulose is a strong, rubbery material that forms the walls of all the **cells** that make up a plant. Leaves, stems, flowers, fruits and roots all contain cellulose. Plant cells are too small to see and so you cannot see all the fibre in a plant, but some plants contain hard or stringy parts that are easy to see. Celery and rhubarb, for example, are stems and they have stringy bits that run from one end to the other. Seeds, particularly beans and grains, are often protected with a tough outer skin that is rich in cellulose. The skin of an apple, for example, or a potato, contains more fibre than the rest of it.

Digesting cellulose

Cellulose is a carbohydrate that cows, sheep and other grazing animals can digest. Humans, however, cannot digest cellulose because the human digestive system does not contain the **enzymes** (change catalysts) that are needed to break it down. So, although fibre is mainly carbohydrate, eating it does not give you any **energy**.

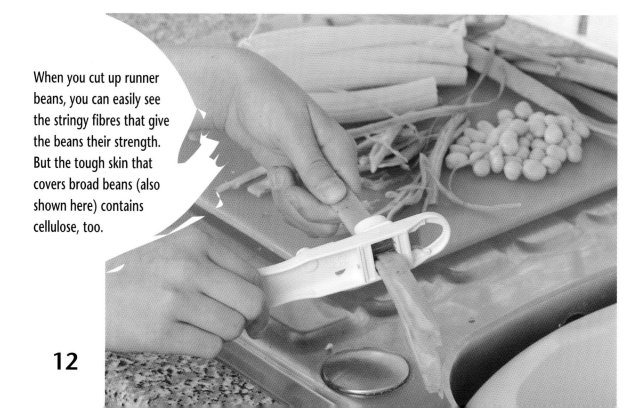

When you cut up runner beans, you can easily see the stringy fibres that give the beans their strength. But the tough skin that covers broad beans (also shown here) contains cellulose, too.

Chlorophyll gives plant its green colour

Nucleus controls cell

Cell wall made of cellulose

Space filled with plant sap

The walls of plant cells are made of cellulose. Some parts of the plant have thick cell walls containing extra cellulose.

Chewing

Because cellulose is so tough, it is difficult to chew. It takes longer, for example, to chew up a mouthful of raw carrot than it does to chew a piece of chocolate. And, after chewing, you have more to swallow. Chewing helps your digestive system because it breaks up the food into smaller pieces before you swallow it, making it easier to digest. In addition, the more you chew, the more **saliva** your mouth makes, and saliva contains an enzyme that starts to digest other carbohydrates.

Soluble fibre

Soluble fibre includes pectins and gums found in fruits such as apples and vegetables, such as turnips and sweet potatoes. It is also present in oats. Soluble fibre in the diet can help to reduce the amount of cholesterol in the blood.

Fibre in food

Although you can clearly see stringy bits in many vegetables, the foods that are richest in fibre are nuts, dried fruit, beans, lentils and peas, and foods made from grains, such as rice and wheat, which are made into bread and pasta. Rice and wheat, however, are often processed so that most of the fibre is taken out of them. This is called 'refining'.

Nuts and dried fruit

Nuts are the seeds of some trees. They include coconuts, hazel nuts, walnuts, almonds and pine nuts. Nuts are rich in fibre, **protein** and vegetable oil, which is a kind of **fat**. Dried fruits include dates, prunes and desiccated (dried out) coconut. Raisins, sultanas and currants are all different kinds of dried grapes.

Pulses

Pulses are seeds from pods, such as beans, lentils and peas, and are rich in protein as well as in fibre. They are among the healthiest foods you can eat, because they contain almost no fat. Most children like to eat baked beans and peas. Other pulses are made into tasty dishes. The Indian food dahl is made from lentils mixed with spices and the dip houmous is made mainly from chickpeas.

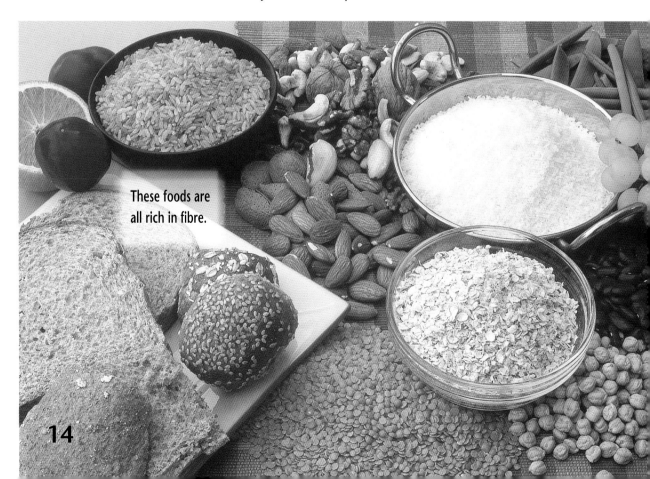

These foods are all rich in fibre.

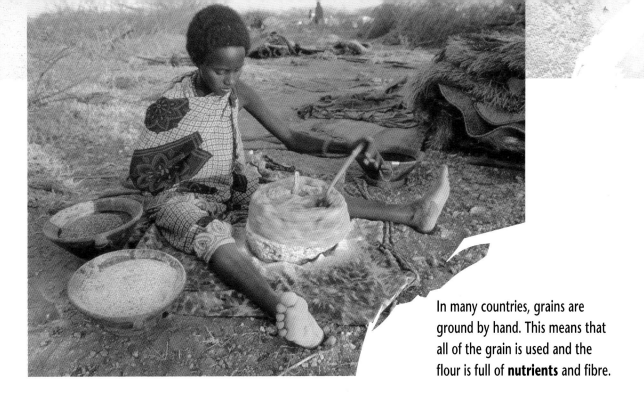

In many countries, grains are ground by hand. This means that all of the grain is used and the flour is full of **nutrients** and fibre.

Grains

Grains come from cereal crops, such as wheat, rice, oats, maize and barley. Breakfast cereals, as the name suggests, are made from cereal grains. The grains we eat most are wheat and rice. Wheat is ground into flour that is used to make bread, pasta, cakes and biscuits. Rice is normally eaten as a grain with meat or vegetables. How much fibre we get from grains depends on how much of the grain is used in the food. Brown rice and wholegrain foods use all of the grain and so contain more fibre than white rice and refined flour.

Wholegrain and refined foods

Wholemeal flour is ground from whole grains of wheat and is made into wholemeal bread, wholemeal pasta and other wholemeal products. Most white flour, pasta and white bread is made from wheat from which much of the fibre has been removed. All bread and pasta, however, contains some fibre.

Food with no fibre

Many foods contain almost no fibre at all. Milk and other dairy products, meat and fish contain no natural fibre. Many other foods, such as chocolate, fizzy drinks, some cakes and biscuits have had all or almost all the fibre taken out.

Brown bread or wholemeal?
Most wholemeal breads are brown, but not all brown breads are wholemeal. You have to look on the wrapping to see how much fibre a loaf of bread contains.

What happens in the digestive system?

The job of the digestive system is to break up the **nutrients** in food into pieces that are small enough to pass through the walls of the gut and into the bloodstream. **Carbohydrates**, **fats** and **proteins** are broken down into separate **molecules**, and even, in the case of protein, into parts of molecules. Water molecules are so small they pass easily into the blood, but with fibre the opposite is true. It cannot be broken down small enough and so is not absorbed and passes right through the digestive system.

In the mouth

Digestion begins in the mouth. The teeth slice, chop and grind the food into smaller pieces that mix with **saliva** to make a soft mush. Chewing is particularly important in breaking up fibre. It makes the fibre soft and easy to swallow. When the mouthful of food has been chewed enough, your tongue pushes it to the back of your mouth and you automatically swallow it.

In the stomach

The mushy pulp passes down your throat, through the **pharynx** and into the **oesophagus**, the tube that joins your mouth to your stomach. The walls of the stomach make a strong acid, called hydrochloric acid. This acid usually kills off any germs in the food and starts to break the proteins up into separate molecules. Your stomach is a stretchy bag that stores and churns the food for a few hours. The mushy pulp gradually changes into a kind of thick soup, called **chyme**. Every so often, some of the chyme squirts from your stomach into the **small intestine**.

Body fact

In adults, the length of the digestive tube from the mouth to the anus is about 9.5 metres long. In children it is shorter. Multiply your height by 5.5 to get a rough idea of the length of your digestive tube.

In the small intestine

The small intestine is a long thin tube. As chyme passes into the tube, it mixes with digestive juices that come from the **liver**, the **pancreas** and the walls of the small intestine. The juice from the pancreas **neutralizes** the acid of the stomach juice. This lets the **enzymes** in all the digestive juices get to work on the food, breaking up the carbohydrates, proteins and fats. Gradually these nutrients pass through the walls of the small intestine into the blood. The remainder, mainly fibre, digestive juices and water, passes from the small intestine into a wider tube called the **large intestine**.

The digestive system breaks up food using mechanical and chemical processes. It changes the food from a bite-sized chunk of, for example, peanut butter sandwich into a mushy pulp and then into a soupy liquid.

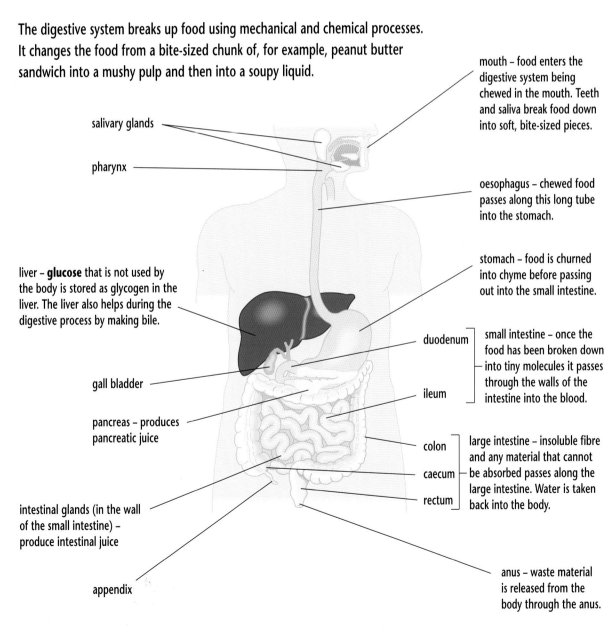

salivary glands

pharynx

liver – **glucose** that is not used by the body is stored as glycogen in the liver. The liver also helps during the digestive process by making bile.

gall bladder

pancreas – produces pancreatic juice

intestinal glands (in the wall of the small intestine) – produce intestinal juice

appendix

mouth – food enters the digestive system being chewed in the mouth. Teeth and saliva break food down into soft, bite-sized pieces.

oesophagus – chewed food passes along this long tube into the stomach.

stomach – food is churned into chyme before passing out into the small intestine.

duodenum

small intestine – once the food has been broken down into tiny molecules it passes through the walls of the intestine into the blood.

ileum

colon

caecum

rectum

large intestine – insoluble fibre and any material that cannot be absorbed passes along the large intestine. Water is taken back into the body.

anus – waste material is released from the body through the anus.

Digesting water and fibre

Water passes easily through the walls of the digestive system into the blood. Some of it is absorbed in the stomach, but more is absorbed in the **small intestine**. The rest combines with fibre to form a mushy paste that passes into the **large intestine**. Here more water is absorbed through the walls of the tube and the paste gradually becomes more solid.

Fibre in the small intestine

Carbohydrates are broken up in the mouth, in the stomach and in the small intestine. Fibre, however, is not able to be digested and absorbed in the small intestine and passes largely unchanged into the large intestine.

Fibre in the large intestine

The undigested fibre travels slowly through the large intestine and forms one of the main components of **faeces**. Faeces, however, is not simply fibre and water. It also contains digestive juices, **mucus**, dead **cells** from the walls of the digestive system and **bacteria** from the large intestine.

The wall of the small intestine is lined with tiny bumps called villi. They give the small intestine a bigger area for absorbing nutrients.

Hostile environment

The digestive system is a hostile and harsh environment. The **enzymes** and acid in the juices, which break down food so efficiently, can also attack the living cells of the digestive system itself. The walls of the stomach and intestines are protected by mucus. The lining of the stomach and intestine have a rapid turnover of cells, which means the cells only last a few days. As the cells die, they join the undigested waste.

Water

As water is absorbed through the lining of the stomach and intestine it can carry with it water soluble **vitamins** and **minerals**. More water is absorbed in the large intestine. Provided the body is not short of water, enough remains in the large intestine to make the faeces soft and moist.

Getting rid of faeces

Of all the food you eat, only a small fraction completes the whole journey through the digestive system. Faeces are stored at the end of the large intestine. It moves from here into the rectum and is then expelled from the body through the anus. A tight muscle in the anus relaxes to allow the faeces to pass through.

This high magnification scan shows the mucus lining of the large intestine. The mucus helps the faeces move and protects the intestine wall from damage.

Time in transit

Most undigested food takes about ten hours to reach the large intestine. It may take up to another 20 hours before it finally leaves the body.

Using fibre

Most fibre is **insoluble fibre**. It is not digested and passes through the intestines with all the other waste matter. Fibre makes the waste matter, called **faeces**, bulkier. Bulky faeces helps the **large intestine** – also called the bowel – to work better and helps to keep it healthy. Some fibre is **soluble**.

A long and winding journey

The **small intestine** is coiled within the folds of the large intestine. Food has to make its way through all the coils into the large intestine. Undigested food and waste then have to travel upwards – against gravity – along and down to reach the anus, the final exit. The process by which food and waste are moved through the digestive tubes is called 'peristalsis'.

Peristalsis

The walls of the gut contain circular bands of muscles. When a band of muscle contracts it pushes the food forwards. At the same time, the band of muscle in front of the food relaxes, allowing the food to slide through it. The movement of each muscle relaxing and then contracting passes along the tube like a wave. The muscles in the small intestines work continually, churning the food around the tube, but the muscles in the large intestine work much more slowly.

Peristalsis fact
Peristalsis moves food through the digestive system whatever position your body is in. This means that even if you are upside-down you can still digest food.

Healthy bowels

Fibre makes the waste bulkier and this gives the muscles of the intestines more to push against. They therefore work more often and more efficiently. If you eat plenty of fibre and drink plenty of water you are likely to empty your bowels about once a day. This keeps the muscles of the large intestine healthy, and stops **bacteria** and stale waste building up inside the bowels. Some people go to the toilet more often and some people go less often than once a day. What matters most is that the waste material is bulky and easy to push out of the body.

Absorbing cholesterol

Oats and certain fruits and vegetables contain **soluble fibre**. It can bind to bile acids that are released into the small intestine to help digest fat in the diet. The bile acids bound to soluble fibre then cannot be reabsorbed and recycled for further use. Instead they pass into the large intestine were they form part of the faeces. This means that more cholesterol in the blood is needed to be converted into new bile acids. This is how soluble fibre in the diet helps lower blood cholesterol levels.

Muscles contract behind mushy solids

Bands of muscles

Muscles relax in front of mushy solids

Valve between **oesophagus** and stomach

Valve between stomach and small intestine

Valve between small and large intestines

Food moves through all the tubes in the digestive system in much the same way as you squeeze toothpaste out of a tube. Valves separate one stage of the digestion system from the next. They allow food to travel only in one direction.

Water in the body

Water is the main ingredient of all the different fluids in the body, including digestive juices, blood, sweat and **urine**. Each of these liquids needs water to make them runny. In addition, all the **organs** and tissues inside your body are coated with moisture. Salty water inside and outside the **cells** allows **nutrients** and chemicals to enter and leave each cell. Water is also involved in many of the chemical reactions that take place inside the body.

Digestive juices

Digestive juices, produced in the **liver** and **pancreas**, trickle through narrow tubes and into the **small intestine**. They join other digestive juices made in the mouth, stomach and in the walls of the intestines.

Hitching a ride

Minerals, such as salt, and some **vitamins** can only be taken into the body along with water. They **dissolve** in water and pass with it into the blood.

Blood

The clear, watery part of blood is called plasma. This clear liquid has sugar and other nutrients dissolved in it. Red blood cells take in **oxygen** in the lungs. As the blood circulates around the body, every living cell is provided with a constant supply of food and oxygen.

Drinking plenty of water helps to keep your skin moist and healthy. It also helps all the cells in your body work better.

Water in the cells

Water plays an important role in helping nutrients and oxygen pass from the blood into each cell. Chemical reactions inside the cells change **glucose** and oxygen into **energy**, while other reactions allow the cell to carry out its own particular tasks. Many of these chemical reactions involve water. Water then helps **carbon dioxide** and waste chemicals pass from the cell into the blood to be taken away and expelled from the body.

Urine and sweat

Waste chemicals are carried away from the cells by the blood and out of the body in urine or sweat. Urine is made in the kidneys (see pages 26 and 27), while sweat is made in the sweat glands and is pumped out of the body through tiny holes in the skin. Although you are only aware of sweating when you are very hot or the air is very moist, you are actually sweating all the time. Sweat consists mainly of water with salt and other waste chemicals dissolved in it.

Some parts of the body contain more water than other parts. This chart shows the percentage of water in different parts of the body. Surprisingly, the water content of the brain is higher than that of blood.

Water fact
Your body produces 10 litres of digestive juices every day. Most of this is water that is reabsorbed into the body.

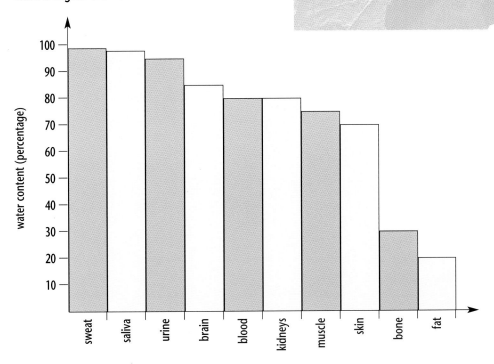

Water balance

Your body loses water all the time. It loses water just from breathing, but it loses most water in the form of **urine** and sweat (see pages 22 and 23). Altogether, you probably lose about 2–3 litres of water a day. To replace the water lost, you take in new supplies of water every day in your food and by drinking. Your body has to balance the water lost with the water taken in.

Urine

Nearly half of all the water you lose is urine. How much urine your kidneys make depends on how much water you have drunk and how hot the weather is. The more you drink the more urine you make. However, when you are hot you lose more water as sweat. To keep the amount of water in your body balanced, your kidneys then produce less urine.

Sweating

Your body loses water through the skin all the time, but when you are hot you sweat much more. Sweating helps to cool your body down. The water is pumped on to your skin, but the heat of your body makes it **evaporate**. As it evaporates it takes heat from your blood.

Breathing out

When blood reaches your lungs, **carbon dioxide** and water **vapour** pass from the blood into the lungs. These two gases then leave the body with the air that you breathe out. Every day you breathe out the equivalent of 500 millilitres of water in the form of vapour.

If you breathe out on to a mirror, the mirror will mist up with water droplets. These droplets have **condensed** from water vapour in the air that you have just breathed out.

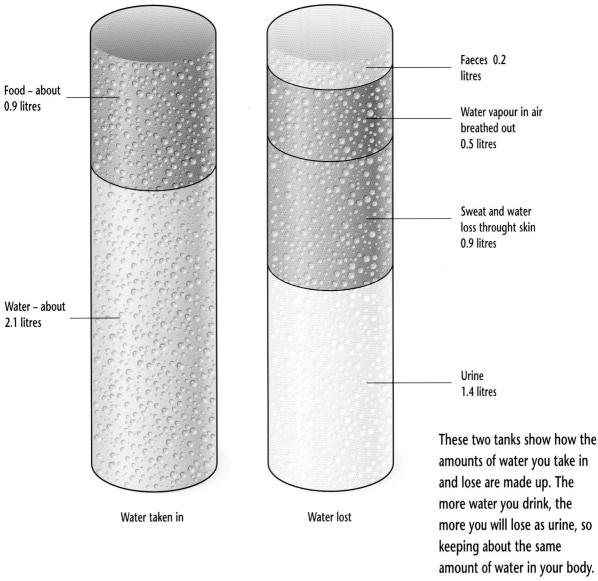

Food – about
0.9 litres

Water – about
2.1 litres

Faeces 0.2
litres

Water vapour in air
breathed out
0.5 litres

Sweat and water
loss throught skin
0.9 litres

Urine
1.4 litres

Water taken in

Water lost

These two tanks show how the amounts of water you take in and lose are made up. The more water you drink, the more you will lose as urine, so keeping about the same amount of water in your body.

Faeces

Faeces contains water as well as fibre and waste materials. The water in faeces makes it soft and easier to push out of the body. Usually only about 6 per cent of water lost is in faeces but, if you have **diarrhoea**, a lot of extra water and salts may be lost. If you are suffering from diarrhoea, it is important to drink extra water to make up for that lost.

Thirst

Thirst is a strong signal that your body needs more water to balance the water lost. You feel thirsty when your mouth becomes drier because it is making less **saliva**. By this time, your body is really short of water. You should drink regularly throughout the day, so that your body does not have to send you this emergency signal!

Water in the kidneys

You have two kidneys, one on each side of the body just above your waist. They filter the blood and remove poisonous waste, such as **urea**, and excess water and salt. The water with salt and urea **dissolved** in it trickles from the kidneys down to the bladder, where it is stored.

Poisonous waste

The main ingredient of urea is **nitrogen**. The **liver** changes the body's waste nitrogen into urea, a solid that **dissolves** easily in the water in the blood. The liver also breaks down other poisons in the body and turns them into harmless waste chemicals. These include chemicals that you would not usually think of as poisons, for example, caffeine in cola.

In the kidneys

Each kidney is made up of over a million tiny filters. As blood enters a filter, water and everything dissolved in it is forced out of the blood. Most of the water and all the dissolved food and **nutrients** pass through the filter and back into the blood. What is left over is excess water with urea, salt and waste chemicals dissolved in it. It is called **urine** and it trickles down one of the tubes, called ureters, into the bladder.

Vein carries purified blood back to heart

Artery brings blood to kidneys

Nephrons filter blood

Kidneys

Kidneys

Ureters

Ureter carries urine to bladder

Bladder

Urethra

About a quarter of your blood passes through your kidneys every minute. The kidneys clean the blood by filtering out poisonous chemicals and excess salt and water. This produces urine, which is stored in the bladder.

Excess water

You may think that drinking extra water will make your kidneys work harder, but in fact extra water makes it easier for your kidneys. The more water there is in your blood, the more diluted the excess salt and other wastes become. This means that each filter has to deal with less.

Urine

The kidneys send a constant trickle of urine into the bladder, where it is stored. As the bladder fills up with urine, it stretches. Nerves in the walls of the bladder alert your brain when you need to urinate. If you wait until your bladder is very full, the need to urinate will become desperate. The more liquid you drink, the more often you need to urinate.

Urinating

A ring of muscle at the bottom of the bladder usually keeps the bladder tightly closed. When you urinate, this muscle relaxes and urine flows out of your body from the bladder through a tube called the urethra.

Babies cannot recognize when they need to urinate and cannot control the muscle that allows urine to leave the bladder. They wear nappies to absorb the urine instead.

Bladder fact

Your bladder can hold only about 0.5 litres of urine at a time, but your body makes about three times this amount every day. This means that you have to urinate several times a day.

Too little water

If you do not drink enough water, you become **dehydrated**. This makes it difficult for your body to get rid of the poisonous waste chemicals in your blood. If you do not drink enough for many hours you will become thirstier and thirstier as your body becomes increasingly desperate for water. People can survive only for a few days without water.

Dehydration

You would expect that the first sign of dehydration would be feeling thirsty, but this is not always so. When your body is short of water, your kidneys cannot clean your blood of all the poisons in it. Extra poisons in the blood can cause lots of different symptoms. They can make you feel tired, dizzy and lacking in energy. They can also cause headaches and stop you sleeping well at night.

Sweating

Sweating also causes dehydration, so you should always drink more liquid in hot weather or when you are in a hot place. Athletes and other people who are exercising vigorously can lose up to 1.7 litres of sweat an hour and are particularly in danger of dehydration.

Tennis players often have to play hard in very hot weather. Players sip water in the breaks between games so they will not become dehydrated.

Severe dehydration

When someone suffers from severe dehydration, all of the tissues in their body become short of water and cannot function properly. Their heart starts to beat very fast and their **blood pressure** falls. If they do not get treatment they will go into **shock** and die.

Dying of thirst

When you think of someone dying of thirst, you probably think of people stranded at sea or lost in the desert, but millions of people worldwide die of dehydration every year. Most of these deaths are due to dysentery, an infectious disease that causes severe **diarrhoea**. Other people die of dehydration when they lose a lot of blood or suffer burns that cover a large area of their body.

Annalise's story

Annalise drank very little during the day, because she didn't like using the school toilets. Her skin was dry, she often had headaches and felt tired and listless. Then she read in the newspaper that these problems could be caused by dehydration. She carried a bottle of water to drink during the day. When she got home she drank lots of water. Her headaches have gone, she now feels more energetic and her skin is no longer dry.

This person has been in an accident and lost a lot of blood. The hospital has put her on a drip – a mixture of water, **glucose** and salts. It is fed into her blood to stop her becoming dehydrated.

Too much water

In normal circumstances it is quite difficult to drink too much water. When you have drunk about a litre, your stomach will be full and you will not want to drink any more. The people who are most likely to drink too much water are those who are trying to avoid **dehydration**. When a person becomes overheated, they may overcorrect and drink far too much liquid. Too much water upsets the balance of water and salt in the body and, in extreme cases, can cause death.

Balancing water and salt

Salt controls how much water passes out of the blood into your tissues to keep them moist. Your kidneys normally make sure that your blood contains the right amount of salt and water. But if the blood contains too much water and not enough salt, water leaves the blood and floods the tissues of the body.

Overheating

Athletes and, more dangerously, people who take the illegal drug ecstasy are most at risk of overheating. When you become hot, your body sweats to cool you down. Sweat includes salt and water, so when you sweat your body loses both. Sweating usually keeps your temperature more or less constant, but sometimes people become so hot sweating cannot cool them. Highly trained athletes should know how much water they need to drink to prevent overheating, but the drug ecstasy makes people think that everything is all right with the world, even when things are going dangerously wrong.

Drinking water usually helps your kidneys to work better, but, if your kidneys cannot cope with it, excess water may flood your body.

Flooded with water

Several ecstasy users have died from drinking too much water when they were overheated. Ecstasy users are in danger of becoming dehydrated. But, if they drink pint after pint of water, the amount of salt in the body becomes too diluted. The drug ecstasy also stops the kidneys working. Instead of the extra water being extracted from the blood, it floods their tissues. Most damaging, their brain becomes swollen. As it swells it is squashed by the bony skull that usually protects it. Pressure on the brain quickly leads to **coma** and death.

Safe amount to drink

Athletes, and anyone who is exercising vigorously or liable to become very hot, should drink about half a litre an hour. Sipping water or soft drinks will replace the water lost. Isotonic drinks, which are special drinks for athletes, are the best things to sip, since they include salts.

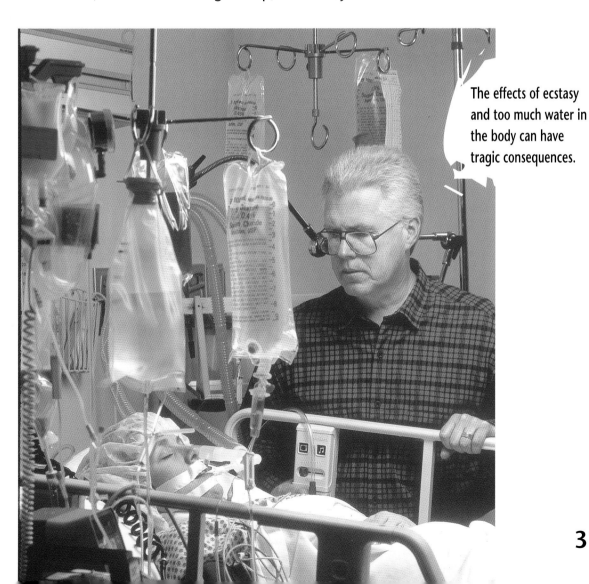

The effects of ecstasy and too much water in the body can have tragic consequences.

Too little fibre

If you do not eat enough fibre, your **large intestine** will work slowly and sluggishly. The immediate effect of this is to cause constipation, which is difficulty in passing **faeces**. Over a long period of time, continual constipation leads to piles and possibly cancer of the large intestine.

Moving along

If your food does not contain much fibre, very little passes undigested into the bowel (another name for the large intestine). Undigested food only moves through the bowel when the muscles of the tube tighten behind it and push it forward. The less undigested food there is in the large intestine, the less often the muscles contract. This means that undigested food stays in the bowel for much longer than it should.

These foods contain almost no fibre. Only the tomato and the bun contain a little fibre. If you like to eat food like this, you should also include foods that are high in fibre, such as baked beans, wholemeal bread and vegetables.

Constipation

How easy it is to push faeces out of the body depends on how much fibre and water they contain. The longer the mushy paste stays in the bowel, the more water from it is absorbed back into the body. This means that the waste material becomes dry and hard, which makes it difficult and painful to push it out of the body.

Testing transit time

Transit time is the time taken for undigested food to pass right through your body. It should be between 12 and 24 hours. You can test your transit time by eating a lot of beetroot – it will dye your faeces red! See how long it takes for the undigested beetroot to pass out of your body. If it is more than 24 hours, you need to eat more fibre and drink more water.

Relieving constipation

If you often suffer from constipation, you should eat more fibre and drink more water. A glass of luke-warm water first thing in the morning often helps. You can buy remedies for constipation from the chemist, but you should not use them all the time.

Piles

Constipation is unpleasant and can build up trouble for the future. Adults who often suffer from constipation may develop piles. The blood vessels in the anus and rectum become stretched and swollen, like varicose veins. Piles are itchy and are painful, particularly when passing faeces.

Cancer of the bowel

Continual constipation over many years can lead to cancer of the bowel. People who live in Europe, Australia and North America are more likely to get cancer of the bowel than people who live in Africa and Asia. This is because most Africans and Asians have far more fibre in their diets.

Eating meals that contain plenty of fibre keeps the large intestine healthy and working well.

Too much fibre

Fibre in your diet makes your digestive system work more efficiently. Eating more fibre than you are used to can cause excess gas to build up, giving you wind and even **diarrhoea**. Too much fibre can also stop you getting enough **nutrients** if it fills your stomach and stops you eating more nutritious food. Some fibre actually prevents particular **minerals** being absorbed into the blood.

Gas in the large intestine

Adults normally have about 200 millilitres of gases in the digestive system, children have a bit less. These gases come from various sources. Some of them are produced in the **large intestine**. There billions of **bacteria** produce **methane**, **carbon dioxide** and **hydrogen** as they feed on the undigested food. These gases have a foul smell and may be passed as wind or when you go to the toilet.

Indigestion

Fibre is difficult to digest, so if you eat a lot of it, your system may be unable to digest it all, giving you indigestion. More undigested food in the large intestine gives the bacteria there more to feed on and so they produce more gas. Some foods, such as beans, cabbage, cauliflower, onions and garlic, make more gas than others. The extra gases fill the digestive tube, making your **abdomen** sore and swollen. Chewing your food for longer helps to prevent indigestion and reduces excess wind.

This girl has just eaten a meal that contained too much fibre. Now her abdomen is sore because her intestines are swollen with gas.

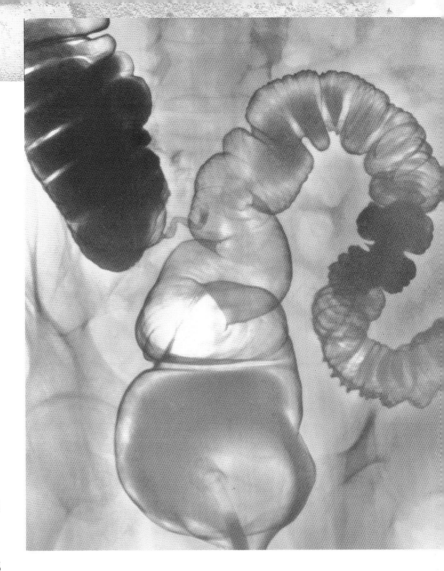

Intestines can become inflamed and cause discomfort if the wrong amount of fibre is eaten.

Irritable gut

Too much fibre can make your digestive tubes inflamed and irritable. Apart from causing pain, food is pushed through the intestines too quickly, so there is not enough time for the water to be absorbed through the wall of the large intestine into the blood. Extra water in the faeces makes it very loose and runny, producing diarrhoea.

Replacing nutrients

Young children in particular should not eat too much fibre because it might replace nutritious food. It fills their stomach so that they stop eating before they have taken in enough **carbohydrates**, **fats**, **proteins** and other nutrients.

Minerals

The fibre contained in the outer skins of wholemeal cereals prevents some minerals, particularly **calcium**, **iron** and **zinc**, from being absorbed into the blood. Children in particular should not eat a lot of raw bran.

Gas in the stomach

Most of the gas in your stomach is air that you swallow with your food and carbon dioxide from fizzy drinks. If there is too much gas in your stomach, you usually burp to get rid of some of it.

Healthy eating

Just as it is important to eat enough, but not too much, fibre, it is also important to eat enough, but not too much, of each kind of **nutrient** – **carbohydrates**, **proteins**, **fats**, **vitamins** and **minerals**. Eating the right amount of all these kinds of foods means you have a balanced diet.

Balance of Good Health

Different kinds of foods are rich in different nutrients. The 'Balance of Good Health' plate divides food into five main groups. It shows the kinds of food you should eat most of, and the kinds you should only eat a little of.

1 – Bread, other cereals and potatoes

These foods are rich in carbohydrates and so give you **energy**. About a third of all the food you eat should come from this group. If you choose wholemeal bread, pasta and flour, you will get lots of fibre, too. Muesli and porridge oats are two breakfast cereals that contain a good quantity of fibre, but do not eat too many of those that contain bran.

2 – Fruit and vegetables

Fruit and vegetables are rich in vitamins, minerals and fibre. Fruit and vegetables should make up another third of your diet. Try to eat at least five portions of fruit and vegetables every day. All types of fruit and vegetables count towards this amount.

3 – Meat, fish and alternatives

This group includes eggs and **pulses**, as well as meat and fish. These foods are all rich in protein, but, apart from pulses, they contain no fibre. Nevertheless, protein is very important, particularly for children who are still growing. You can easily make up the fibre from other kinds of food.

4 – Milk and dairy foods

Milk and dairy foods – cheese, butter, cream and yoghurt – are rich in protein, vitamins and minerals (particularly **calcium**) , although many contain quite a lot of fat and no fibre. It is important to eat some dairy food every day, but, if you are overweight, you should choose special varieties that are lower in fat, such as semi-skimmed milk and low-fat yoghurts.

5 – Food full of fat or sugar

Fatty and sugary foods include chocolate, sweets, cakes, sausages, crisps, fizzy drinks and many other popular snacks. They have little or no fibre. Too much sugar and fat is bad for your health, so you should eat only a very small amount of these foods.

Rules for healthy eating
- Eat a wide variety of food.
- Eat most food from groups 1 and 2.
- Eat only a little food from group 5.

The 'Balance of Good Health' divides food into five main groups. This plate shows which groups you should eat most food from and which groups you should eat the least food from.

Fruit and vegetables

Bread, other cereals and potatoes

Meat, fish, eggs and pulses

Milk and dairy foods

Fatty and sugary foods

Healthy drinking

Your body loses up to 3 litres of liquid a day, mostly in the form of **urine** and sweat. You need to take in enough water to replace the amount lost. Your body gets nearly a third of the water it needs from food but the rest must come from drinks. This means that most people should drink about 2 litres a day.

Water in food and drinks

If you follow the 'balance of good health', you will absorb water from the fruit and vegetables you eat every day, as well as from bread, pasta, rice and potatoes. All food has some water in it, otherwise it would be too dry to eat.

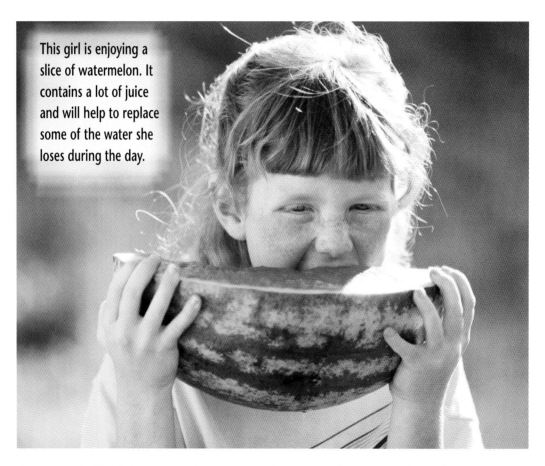

This girl is enjoying a slice of watermelon. It contains a lot of juice and will help to replace some of the water she loses during the day.

Soup and all drinks are mainly water. Some, such as squash and tea, are made by adding water, but others, such as milk, are already made mainly of water. You can replace the liquid your body loses by drinking fruit juices, lemonade and milk, but it is particularly helpful to your body if you also drink plain water.

Caffeine

Cola, tea and coffee all contain a substance called caffeine. Caffeine speeds up the processes in the body and makes you feel more alert. It also makes your kidneys produce more urine, so they extract more water from your blood. Most people can tolerate a certain amount of caffeine without becoming dehydrated. However, when you consume more caffeine than you are used to this can cause mild dehydration.

Alcohol

Alcohol in large amounts can be **dehydrating**. People who have drunk a lot of alcohol often suffer from a hangover afterwards. Their mouth feels dry, their head may ache and they may feel tired and sick. Most of these symptoms are caused by **dehydration** – just one of many problems caused by drinking alcohol.

Current advice from the government on drinking alcohol is that men should drink no more than three units per day and women should drink no more than two units per day. A unit of alcohol is equivalent to half a pint of beer, a small glass of wine or one measure of spirits. Pregnant women should avoid drinking alcohol, especially in the first three months.

The bottle of water shows you how much liquid you should drink every day. The glasses show one way of drinking this amount of liquid. Remember that you cannot count cola, tea or coffee.

Healthy diets

Your diet consists of all the foods you usually eat. Many people in the West, including Europe, Australia and the North America, eat a diet that is too low in fibre. People from other parts of the world eat food that usually contains much more fibre. Vegetarians and vegans follow special diets, but these diets usually contain plenty of fibre.

Traditional diets

Most people in the West use flour refined from wheat, but people in Africa, Asia and South America often make flour from other grains, such as maize and rice, and this flour is less refined. Their diets often include beans, peas or lentils, which are cheap and rich in **nutrients** and fibre. Traditional recipes from these areas are becoming more popular, as people realize how healthy and tasty they are.

Vegetarian and vegan diets

Vegetarians do not eat meat and often do not eat fish either. Vegans exclude any food that has come from animals, including milk and all other dairy food. Vegetarian diets are often more healthy than meat diets because they are more likely to be high in fibre and low in fat. Vegan diets are also usually rich in fibre, but vegans have to choose their food carefully to make sure they get all the nutrients they need.

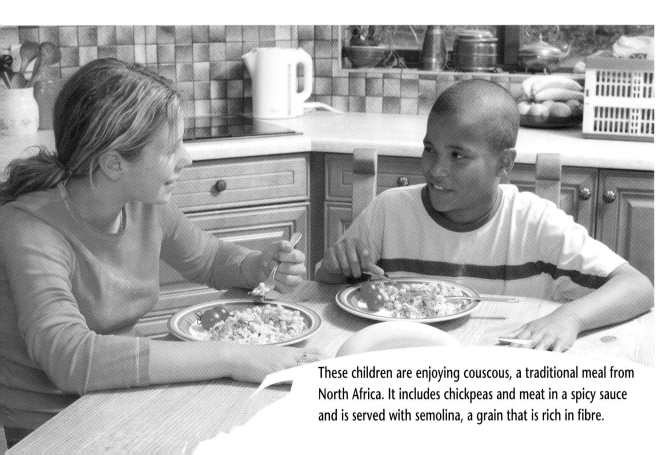

These children are enjoying couscous, a traditional meal from North Africa. It includes chickpeas and meat in a spicy sauce and is served with semolina, a grain that is rich in fibre.

Ben's story

Ben liked to eat chips, sausages, burgers and chocolate, but his doctor told him that he was getting too fat. Ben changed his diet. He stopped eating such fatty food and ate wholemeal bread and spaghetti instead. The fibre in the food stopped him feeling hungry. He also drank plenty of water because the body uses water to break down body fat. When he wanted a snack he had a banana, apple or raw carrot. He joined a sports club at school. He became fitter and healthy, and soon lost all the extra weight.

People who are ill

People who are ill often do not feel like eating very much at all. It is, however, particularly important that they do not stop drinking. If you are vomiting or suffering from **diarrhoea**, you need to drink plenty of water to replace the extra water lost. Similarly, if you have a high temperature, or a fever, you need to drink plenty of extra water to replace all the water lost through sweating.

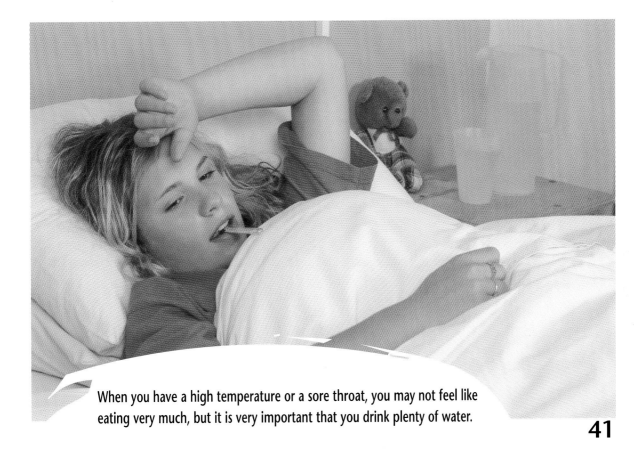

When you have a high temperature or a sore throat, you may not feel like eating very much, but it is very important that you drink plenty of water.

Daily requirements

In the West most people eat about 12 grams of fibre a day, but scientists recommend that adults should have 18 grams a day. Children should have less, depending on their weight. An average man weighs about 73 kilograms, while an average woman weighs about 61 kilograms. If you weigh about half of this (about 33 kilograms) then you should have about 9 grams of fibre,

This meal contains 7.3 grams of fibre and 289 grams of water, that is 289 millilitres, of water.

half the amount for an adult. Young children should have much less fibre. In the same way, while adults should drink about 2 litres of liquid a day, you can reduce this amount if you weigh less.

Food		Amount that gives 10 grams of fibre
Fruit	Apples	3–4 apples
	Bananas	3 bananas
	Oranges	3 oranges
Vegetables	Broccoli	1 large head
	Cabbage	1 medium cabbage
	Carrots	3 carrots
	Coleslaw	1 large serving
Pulses	Baked beans	1 small can
	Lentils	2 cups
	Peas	1 cup
Cereals	Cornflakes	3.5 cups
	Oat cakes	10 biscuits
	Rice crispies	8 cups
	White bread	15 slices
	Wholemeal bread	5 slices
Potatoes	Baked jacket potato	I large
	Boiled new potatoes	7 potatoes

Amount of fibre and water in different foods

Food	Amount of fibre in 100 grams	Amount of water in 100 grams
Apples, including skin	1.8 g	85 ml
Baked beans	3.7 g	72 ml
Baked potatoes	2.7 g	63 ml
Bananas	3.4 g	75 ml
Beetroot	1.9 g	82 ml
Boiled egg	0 g	75 ml
Cheddar cheese	0 g	36 ml
Chocolate	0 g	2 ml
Cooked brown rice	0.8 g	66 ml
Cooked white rice	0.1 g	68 ml
Cooked white spaghetti	1.2 g	73.8 ml
Corn flakes	0.9 g	3 ml
Cottage cheese	0 g	79 ml
Cucumber	0.6 g	96 ml
Desiccated coconut	13.7 g	2 ml
Fish	0 g	65–75 ml
Mango	2.6 g	82 ml
Meat	0 g	40–70 ml
Oranges	1.7 g	86 ml
Oven chips	2 g	59 ml
Peaches	1.7 g	89 ml
Peanut butter	5.4 g	1 ml
Peas	4.7 g	78 ml
Plain sponge cake	0.9 g	20 ml
Raw green pepper	5.1 g	93 ml
Raw mushrooms	1.1 g	92 ml
Raw tomatoes	1 g	93 ml
Runner beans	6.2 g	93 ml
Semi-skimmed milk	0 g	90 ml
Sweet corn	1.4 g	72 ml
Weetabix®	9.7 g	6 ml
White bread	1.5 g	37 ml
Wholemeal bread	5.8 g	38 ml

Glossary

abdomen   belly, the part of the body that contains the stomach and small intestines

amino acids   building blocks of protein. Different amino acids combine together to form a protein.

arteries   tubes that carry blood from the heart to different parts of the body

bacteria   single, living cells. Most kinds of bacteria are harmless, but some kinds can cause disease.

blood pressure   the pressure the blood puts on the walls of the blood vessels as it is pumped round the body. Blood pressure changes depending on the force of the heartbeat.

calcium   simple substance, found in the earth and in foods such as milk and cheese. Your body needs calcium for strong healthy bones and teeth.

carbohydrates   substances in food that your body uses to provide energy. Foods that contain a lot of carbohydrates include bread, rice, potatoes and sugar.

carbon dioxide   one of the gases in the air. Plants and animals breathe out carbon dioxide.

cell   smallest living unit. The body is made up of many different kinds of cells, such as bone cells, blood cells and skin cells.

cellulose   substance that the walls of plants cells are made of

chyme   mushy liquid which passes from the stomach to the small intestine. It is formed from partly digested food mixed with the digestive juices of the stomach.

coma   state of deep sleep from which the patient cannot wake up, that can continue for a long time

condensed   when a gas or a vapour, such as water vapour, cools and changes into a liquid

dehydrated   when the body has less water than it needs

diarrhoea   faeces that are loose and watery

dissolve   when a solid or gas merges with a liquid

element   simple substance which cannot be broken up into any other substances

energy   the ability to do work or to make something happen

enzyme   substance that helps a chemical change take place faster without being changed itself

evaporate   when a solid or a liquid becomes a gas

faeces   undigested food, bacteria, digestive juices and dead cells which are excreted as solid waste

fat   substance that the body can change into energy. A layer of fat under the skin helps to keep the body warm.

fungi   group of living things that includes mushrooms, yeasts and moulds

glucose   a kind of sugar

hydrogen   invisible gas that is one of the gases in the air. Hydrogen combines with other substances to form, for example, water, sugar, proteins and fats.

insoluble fibre   fibre that is unable to dissolve in a liquid

iron   a simple substance found in the earth. Your body needs iron so that red blood cells can carry oxygen

large intestine   the part of the intestines through which undigested food passes after it has left the small intestine

liver   body organ which produces digestive juices

methane   gas that occurs naturally in the earth and is made in the body in the large intestine

mineral   non-living substance found in the ground. Your body needs certain minerals to function healthily.

molecule   smallest part of a substance that can exist and still be that substance

mucus   slimy liquid made in the body

neutralize   to make something neutral, that is, neither acid or alkaline

nitrogen   invisible gas that is the main gas in the air. Nitrogen combines with other substances in all the different tissues in your body.

nutrients   parts of food that your body needs to get energy, to build and repair cells and for the cells to function properly. Nutrients include carbohydrates, fats, proteins, vitamins and minerals.

oesophagus   the tube through which food travels from the mouth to the stomach

organ   part of the body that does a particular job. The heart, stomach and intestines are all organs.

oxygen   invisible gas that is one of the gases in the air. The body needs oxygen in order to break down sugar to form energy.

pancreas   gland which produces various digestive juices that flow through a tube into the small intestine

pesticides   substances that kill insects and other pests

pharynx part of the throat where the tubes to the nose, lungs and stomach begin

phosphorus simple substance that is needed for plants to grow

proteins complex chemicals that the body needs to grow and repair cells

pulses group of foods that includes lentils, peas and beans. Pulses are the seeds of some plants and are rich in protein.

recycled reused, sometimes in another form

saliva watery liquid made by glands in your mouth and the inside of your cheeks

sediments solid particles that collect at the bottom of a container of liquid

shock condition caused by a fall in blood pressure that can lead to a person becoming unconscious

small intestine part of the intestine into which food passes from the stomach to be digested and absorbed into the blood. Undigested food passes right through the small intestine into the large intestine.

soluble fibre fibre that dissolves in water and passes into the blood

urea substance formed from waste material in the liver

urine liquid filtered out of the blood by the kidneys as waste and excreted as a yellowish liquid. Urine consists of urea mixed with excess salt and water.

vapour gas that rises from a liquid or solid

vitamins chemicals that your body needs to stay healthy

zinc mineral that the body needs to grow and to help wounds heal

Resources

Books

Body Focus: The Digestive System Carol Ballard (Heinemann Library, 2003)

DEFRA Manual of Nutrition (HMSO, 1995)

Digesting: How We Fuel the Body Angela Royston (Franklin Watts, 1998)

Websites

www.bbc.co.uk/health/nutrition
Nutrition and healthy living are the subject of this part of the BBC's website.

www.mckinley.uiuc.edu/Handouts/sportsnutrquicktips.html
Tells you about drinking fluid, especially useful if you are an athlete or highly active.

www.mckinley.uiuc.edu/health-info/nutrit/hlthdiet/hifiber.html
Tells you about fibre and gives examples of the amounts of fibre in different kinds of food.

www.naturalfacts.com.au/fibre.html
Tells you about fibre and how it keeps you healthy.

www.NutritionAustralia.org
This is the information service of the Australian Nutrition Foundation.

www.nutrition.org.uk/
Website of the British Nutrition Foundation which gives information on all aspects of diet, including fibre. Click on food and nutrition information to get started.

www.phw.co.uk/hpromo/drugfact
Tells you about water in relation to the drug ecstasy.

Index